Giant Short-Faced Bear

by Julie Murray

Abdo Kids Jumbo is an Imprint of Abdo Kids
abdobooks.com

abdobooks.com

Published by Abdo Kids, a division of ABDO, P.O. Box 398166, Minneapolis, Minnesota 55439.

Printed in the United States of America, North Mankato, Minnesota.

052023

092023

Photo Credits: Alamy, Getty Images, Science Source, Shutterstock, ©Dennis Jarvis p.1/CC-BY-SA 2.0, ©Roman Uchytel p.19

Production Contributors: Teddy Borth, Jennie Forsberg, Grace Hansen
Design Contributors: Candice Keimig, Pakou Moua

Library of Congress Control Number: 2022946804

Publisher's Cataloging-in-Publication Data

Names: Murray, Julie, author.

Title: Giant short-faced bear / by Julie Murray

Description: Minneapolis, Minnesota : Abdo Kids, 2024 | Series: Ice age animals | Includes online resources and index.

Identifiers: ISBN 9781098266356 (lib. bdg.) | ISBN 9781098267056 (ebook) | ISBN 9781098267407 (Read-to-me ebook)

Subjects: LCSH: Animals--Juvenile literature. | Extinct animals--Juvenile literature. | Ice Age--Juvenile literature. | Paleontology--Juvenile literature. | Zoology--Juvenile literature.

Classification: DDC 569--dc23

Table of Contents

Ice Age

An ice age is a period when most of the Earth is covered by sheets of ice. The last ice age began about 100,000 years ago. It lasted until about 12,000 years ago. Some animals became **extinct** during this time in history.

ice
land

Giant Short-Faced Bear

The giant short-faced bear first appeared about 1.6 million years ago.

It lived throughout North America in a range of **habitats**. It could be found in places like grasslands and woodlands.

North America
Europe
Africa
South America

The giant short-faced bear lived up to its name. It was 5 feet (1.5 m) tall at the shoulder. On its hind legs, it stood 11 feet (3.4 m) tall! It could weigh more than 2,000 pounds (907 kg).

short-faced bear

saber-toothed tiger

The giant short-faced bear had a **broad** head and short **snout**. It had shaggy brown fur that covered its body.

modern
brown bear

Unlike modern bears, the giant short-faced bear had very long legs and forward-pointing toes. These things helped it run up to 40 miles per hour (64.4 kph)!

The giant short-faced bear could deliver a deadly bite with its strong jaw. Its teeth were long and sharp. These could easily tear through meat.

Food

The giant short-faced bear ate bison, deer, and horses. It may have also eaten plants. Some scientists believe that the bear was a **scavenger**.

Extinction

The giant short-faced bear became **extinct** about 11,000 years ago. It had to compete with other animals and humans for its food. It could not survive.

More Facts

- The giant short-faced bear could eat up to 35 pounds (15.9 kg) of food each day!
- The first **fossils** were discovered in 1878. They were found at Potter Creek Cave in California.
- The giant short-faced bear's closest relative is the modern speckled bear. It is found in South America.
- A full short-faced bear skeleton is on display at the Field Museum in Chicago, Illinois.

Glossary

broad - wide and large.

extinct - no longer existing.

fossil - the remains or trace of a living animal or plant from a long time ago.

habitat - a place where a living thing is naturally found.

scavenger - an animal that finds and eats dead animals.

snout - the front part of an animal's head that sticks out. The snout includes the nose, mouth, and jaws.

Index

Visit **abdokids.com** to access crafts, games, videos, and more!

Use Abdo Kids code

IGK6356

or scan this QR code!